for Eric Berlin

Street Jam

Evan Hause
(2004)

"z" stroke = a "press" roll, approximately four 32nd notes played with one hand, one stroke.

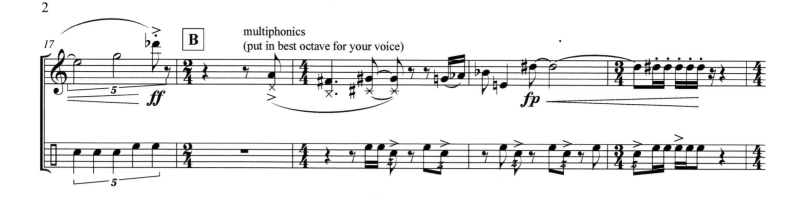

multiphonics
(put in best octave for your voice)

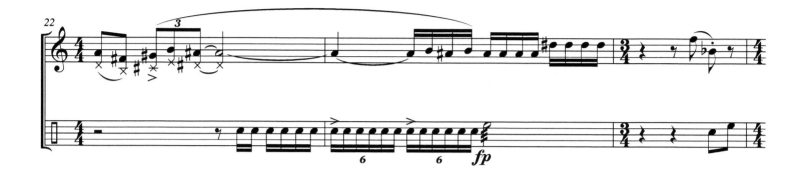

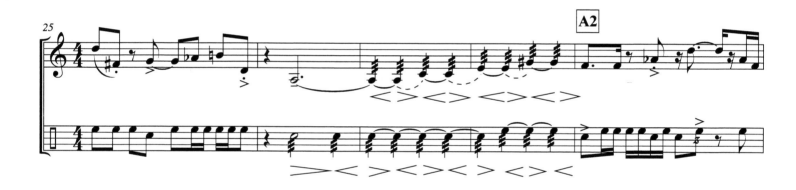

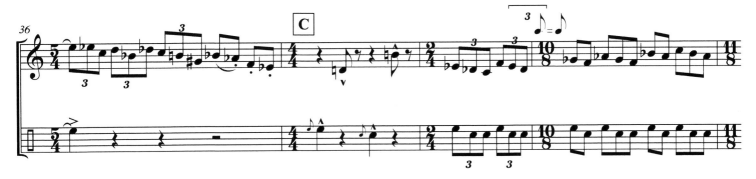

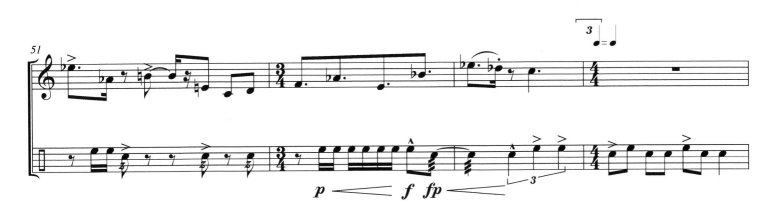

4

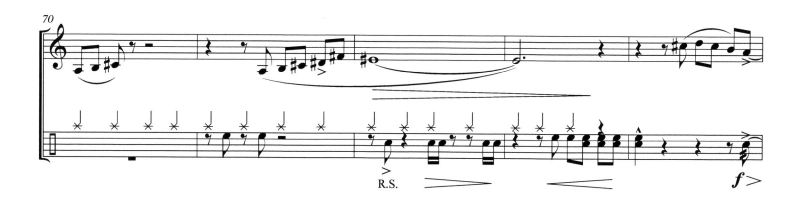

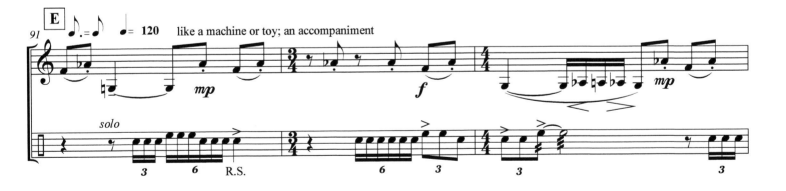

like a machine or toy; an accompaniment

short and spiky

sim.: A♭s short

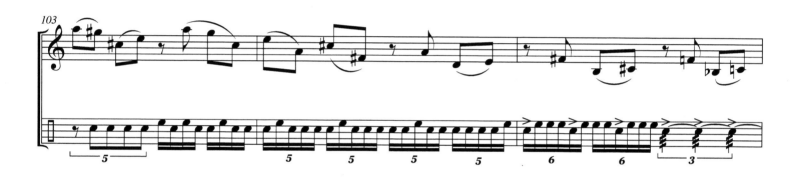

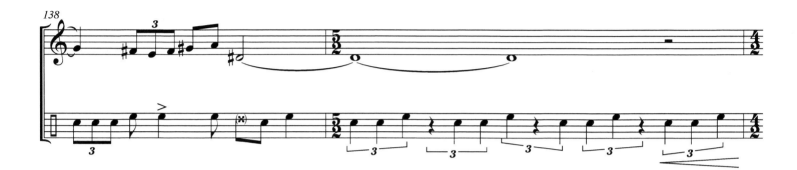

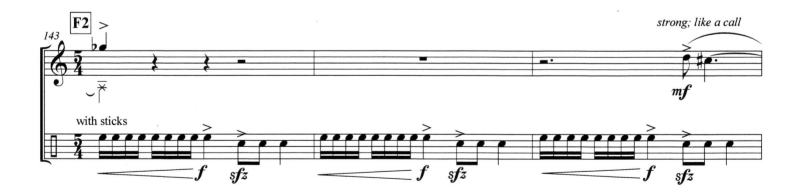

G1 **Free: chant with "talking drum" interjections**

Rit. poco a poco

Free meter. Irregular. *Keep 'em guessing.*
What's coming next? When will it start?
Keep spatial relationship to each other.

Brooklyn, NY
December, 2004

BONGOS

for Eric Berlin

Street Jam

Evan Hause
(2004)

"z" stroke = a "press" roll, approximately four 32nd notes played with one hand, one stroke.

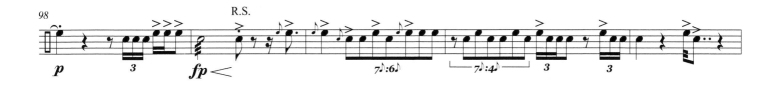

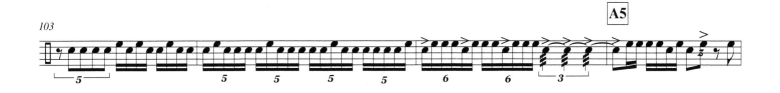

4

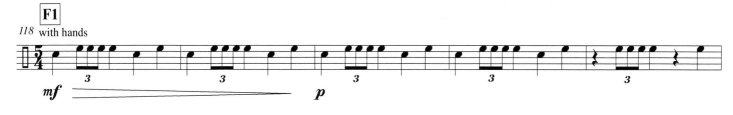

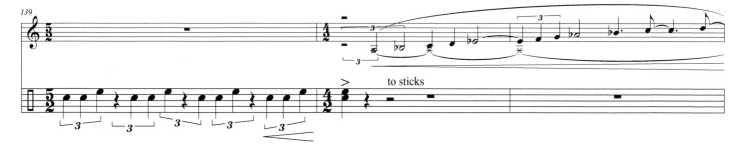

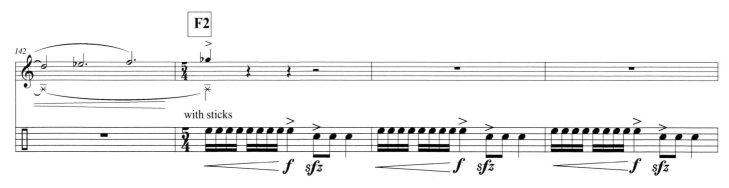

STREET JAM

for Trumpet and Bongos

by

Evan Hause

for Eric Berlin

Street Jam

Evan Hause
(2004)

74

multiphonics

(use the best octave for your voice)

79

85

A4

89

E ♩. = ♪ ♩ = 120

like a machine or toy; an accompaniment

93

short and spiky

sim.: A♭s short

97

102

106

A5

110

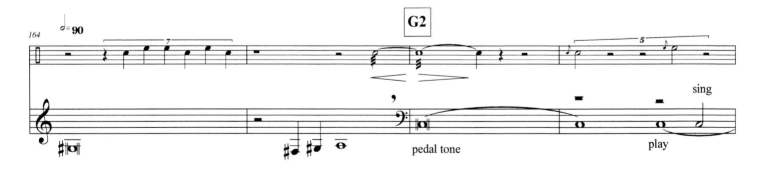

Free meter. Irregular. *Keep 'em guessing.*
What's coming next? When will it start?
Keep spatial relationship to each other.

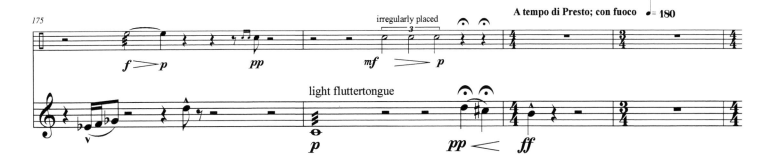

Brooklyn, NY
December 2004

6

Free meter. Irregular. *Keep 'em guessing.*
What's coming next? When will it start?
Keep spatial relationship to each other.

ferocious single-stroke roll

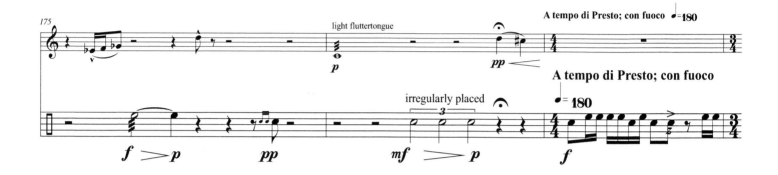

light fluttertongue

A tempo di Presto; con fuoco ♩=180

A tempo di Presto; con fuoco ♩=180

irregularly placed

A6

CODA

(♩=112.5)

Brooklyn, NY
December 2004